The Phoenix Living Poets

———— ∞∞∞∞∞ ————

SAD IRES
and others

SAD IRES

and others

By

D. J. ENRIGHT

CHATTO AND WINDUS

THE HOGARTH PRESS

1975

Published by
Chatto and Windus Ltd
with The Hogarth Press Ltd
42 William IV Street
London WC2

ISBN 0 7011 2134 3

Printed in Great Britain by
Lewis Reprints Ltd.
The Brown Knight and Truscott Group
London and Tonbridge

CONTENTS

Acknowledgments are due to the editors of the following publications, in which some of the poems in this book originally appeared: *Antaeus, Enccunter, The Listener, The London Magazine, New Statesman, Poetry Book Society Christmas Supplement 1973* and *1974, The Times Literary Supplement, Tribune.*

SINCE THEN

So many new crimes since then! —

    simple simony
    manducation of corpses
    infringement of copyright
    offences against the sumptuary laws
    postlapsarian undress
    violation of the Hay-Pauncefote Treaty
    extinction of the dodo
    champerty and malversation
    travelling by public transport without a ticket
    hypergamy and other unnatural practices
    courting in bed
    free verse
    wilful longevity
    dumb insolence
    bootlegging and hijacking
    jackbooting and highlegging
    arsenic and old lace
    robbing a hen-roost
    leaving unattended bombs in unauthorized places
    high dudgeon
    the cod war
    massacre of innocents
    bed-wetting
    escapism
    transporting bibles without a licence

But so many new punishments, too! —

    blinding with science
    death by haranguing
    licking of envelopes
    palpation of the obvious
    invasion of the privacies
    fistula in ano
    hard labour down the minds
    solitary conjunction

mortification of the self-esteem
the Plastic Maiden
hat-rack and trouser-press
the death of a thousand budgerigars
spontaneous combustion
self-employment
retooling of the economy
jacks in orifice
boredom of the genitals
trampling by white elephants
deprivation of forgetfulness
loss of pen-finger
severance pay
strap-hanging
early closing
sequestration of the funny-bone
mortgage and deadlock

"Fair do's," murmured the old Adam, "I am well pleased."
He had come a long way since he named the animals.

IN CEMETERIES

This world a vale of soul-making —
To what intent the finished wares?

Is the ore enforced and fired through
Harsh mills, only to fall aside?

Who is this soulmaster? What say
Do souls have in their made futures?

We mourn the untried young, unmade
In small coffins. What of grown graves?

At times in cemeteries, you hear
Their voices, sad and even-toned,

Almost see the made souls, in their
Curious glory. If you are old.

THE STATIONS OF KING'S CROSS

He is seized and bound by the turnstile.

The moving stair writes once, and
        having writ,
Moves on.

At Hammersmith the nails
At Green Park the tree.

A despatch case which is well named
A square basket made of rattan
Which is a scourge.
The heel of the Serpent bruises Man's instep.

At Earl's Court a Chopper
New, flashing, spotless
It carries hooks and claws and edges
Which wound.

It is hot. Vee
Wipes her face. Cheek to jowl
She wipes the man's on either side.

Rather bear those pills I have
Than fly to others that I know not of.

He speaks to the maidenforms of Jerusalem
Blessed are the paps which never gave suck.

The agony in Covent Garden
He finds them sleeping, for their eyes are heavy.

The first fall, the second fall
The third fall.
And more to come.

A sleeve goes, a leg is torn
A hem is ripped.
This is the parting of garments.

They mock him, offering him vodka.
The effect is shattering.

He is taken down from the strap.
And deposited.

Wilt thou leave him in the loathsome grave?

END OF A DISCOURSE ON THE GENTLE
(OR PERHAPS SLAVISH) MENTALITY

And when you go to the wall
(As you will)
You'll find that even the high one
Around the graveyard
Is no protection.
You lie in the way of a natural by-pass,
Illicit as a sick hedgehog.

And when you get to heaven
(As you will)
Then you'll be told
That you are more to blame than they,
If you hadn't been the way you were
They wouldn't have acted the way they did.

"The Fathers of a city
Lesser though not unlike the present
Ruled that slaves were fit for freedom
Only if enslavement so disgusted them
They took their lives.
We have a rule excluding suicides."

And as you wait there, puzzling it out
(A kind of talk you've heard before
Shuffling your feet as you listened,
Conscious of the justice of it
Paying mute tribute to the rest of it)
They'll push past you at the gate.

"The disposal of this class of souls
Presents as much embarrassment
As does the laying of their bones."

Its own reward,
It will have to be its own reward.

THREE GIRLS

Faith had a fatherless child,
Something had been misplaced.

Charity saw good in everyone,
Until her eyes gave out.

Hope became a chorus girl,
She springs eternally.

Who is the greatest of these?
They are equal. They abide.

REMEMBRANCE SUNDAY

The autumn leaves that strew the brooks
Lie thick as legions.
                    Only a dog limps past,
Lifting a wounded leg.
                    Was it the rocket hurt it?
Asks a child.
                    And next comes Xmas,
Reflects the mother in the silence,
When X was born or hurt or died.

OPEN SESAME

Daughters of memory — in whose company
Alone one forgets, or only remembers
To picture, in strictest epiphany,
Your gay and ever-changing garments . . .

Daughters of memory — how gay and varied
        your garments.
How varied at least. Or your lack of them.
Shyly you arrive, some of you promptly,
Some of you arrive without an appointment . . .

Who summons whom? Who is to feed upon whom?
Some of you seem to be quite hungry.
And not to remember the canon exactly.
Who is intended to leap upon whom?

What can have fathered these pelican daughters?
Their mother a harmless lady, fond of the
        virginal.
Do their fingernails carry diseases?
I have forgotten the word of dismissal.

PREPARING THE LATE ANNE SEXTON
FOR PRESS

Death Notebooks . . . the title's in order.
But we can't have this American spelling —
Look, bombs are in "awful labor",
There's at least one odor,
And a vegetable pocked with·mold.
"What color is the devil?" No saying,
But Death has hair the color of a harp,
While invidious Mr Editor
Sports a cigarette-stained mustache.

"U" to go in, for sure, in this minute
To "Mr Death who stands with his door open".
You went in.

(And what of Mr Life, his use and abuse?
That's a grave subject too.)

Mr Death, she says, was kind to quite a few,
They were quick to be dead,
"But when it comes to my death let it be slow,
Let it be pantomime, this last peep show."

Let it not, thinks Mr Editor, fingering
His cigarette-stained moustache and blue pencil,
Let it not have been.
Mr Funnyman has a funny feeling.

Sad work. Sad cure! — to make a verse of it,
A footnote in the grave. Every blessing's mixed.

DEATH IN A STRANGE LAND

1 *Journalist*

We lunched together on my honeymoon
In Cairo,
A bright boy, *à la page* and mordant,
The whole lot going for him.

Ten years later, in Bangkok,
A trifle apprehensively
(He'd earned himself a reputation,
To burn always with a hard blowlamp flame,
That was his life)
I took him to a favourite smoking place.
Stripping briskly to his underpants
He scared the placid patrons.
It was just the spirit of the thing,
The spirit he was entering into.
The opium burned with a soft sizzling flame.

Some five years passed, we met
In Singapore, at the Cockpit Hotel.
He gave me his review copy, *An Area
Of Darkness,* mine never came to light.
"Always do a long review —
It's the reading takes the time!
We're paid by the word we write, not read."
He'd bought a house in England,
For all his children and one wife,
Under one roof, he said.
After he'd left, the manager rang me
About an unpaid bill, "quite unintentional,
I'm sure."

Three years later, at the Cockpit bar
We shared another easy gin or two
(The bill was surely paid).
He was heading for Vietnam then,
In a hurry.

A few days more, then in *The Times*
A brief obituary —
Found dead in bed,
A hotel in Saigon.

"Strange and outrageous,"
Someone said, I think,
Of his life and death.
The blowlamp had burned right out.
Small mercy anywhere.
From Vietnam the stories still kept coming,
Strange and outrageous.

2 *External Examiner*

He must have found us degenerate,
Our visitor.
We went everywhere by car
(It's hot here, we said, there aren't
Any pavements, and a white man walking
Unnerves the natives),
Ping pong our only exercise
Between beers in the Staff Club,
And all those gins we drank.

At home he played squash twice a week
With a colleague twenty years his junior,
And went for long walks on the moors.

Squash was a better drink as well.
Was it drink that made us effete?
Heat made us thirsty — did heat make us effete?

On the eve of his departure,
The papers marked, honours allotted,
Justice tempered with the usual mercy —
At a Chinese restaurant
(Life's ironies are grosser
Than I could fabricate,
I tell it just the way it was —

Is that excuse enough?),
A place called the Celestial Room,
Midnight and the last mild dance,
He dropped to the floor and died.

After the useless hospital,
The police, the prompt sequestering
Of a British passport
(And some spare cash, I found out later),
I rang his unbelieving widow.
For her a February evening
Dank in England,
For me, three in the morning,
Tropic black, the clockwork crickets,
A gibbon's rending cry.

Tomorrow was his birthday, he'd be back
For that. How could I convince her?
I was not convinced. Except
Outside a Chinese detective shouted
About some suitcase and some keys.
True, her tomorrow was our today.

The first time that I slept,
My dream returned to the restaurant
Exactly as it was,
But now his wife was with us, and a doctor,
So we were less effete.
He fell, exactly as he did. They tended him.
He rose and smiled.
I woke in horror and omission's sin.

But later slept again: the dream resumed its plot,
He fell a second time, and fire consumed him
Every nerve. And neither wife nor doctor
Could assuage that longdrawn agony.

21

I woke again, in different horror.
But then remembered it the way it was,
And how death came as kindly as it could,
With quite unusual mercy.
Dreams, they say, tell stories
To explain away our woes,
And so we go on living.

ORIGIN OF THE HAIKU

The darkness is always visible
Enough for us to write.
We pass the time composing *haiku*.
It concentrates the mind —

Counting every syllable,
Revising, counting again.
A lot of thought goes into 17 syllables,
A lot of time, and (you might say)
A lot of pain.

Once a desperate faction
Proposed to bring in rhyme,
A trick for using up more time —
They lost by a large majority.
We are a conventional lot,
This is a conventional spot,
And we take some satisfaction
In writing verse called *free*.

In between we make up epigrams.
"Not to know me argues yourselves unknown",
Or "What is else not to be overcome?"
The mind is sometimes its own place.

Such petty projects —
Yes, but even an epic,
Even *Paradise Lost,*
Would look puny
In hell, throughout eternity.
It's the taking of pains that counts.

Even here, you will see,
There are manners.
After all, we live in society.
There are long periods set aside
For conversation —
Well no, not the weather,
But the world situation,
The events in Vietnam, Ulster,
Whatever's going.
Who do you think invented politics,
And why? At times I fancy
That is why the world was created —
For our benefit all that
Life and time. What else
To chat about in eternity?

Of course it's wearisome.
Like a cocktail party, minus
The means to get high
Or go home.
But no one can suffer all the time.
There's so much of it —
Time, I mean.

Oh you'll know when you're suffering,
No doubt about it.
It's considered a private thing,
Almost discreditable,
Nobody talks about it.
Neuroses and illnesses
At least were distinguishable.
These pains are the same,
Nobody wants to know.
Maybe you didn't live alone,
Maybe you didn't die alone,
But this you will do alone.
No one wants to hear a word about it,
No one will listen.

Perhaps that's the worst part of all.
— But I have gone too far,
You must forget that I said that.
Only remember,
It is best not to think,
Except about Vietnam, about Ulster.
I do not say they are small mercies,
I do not think they are mercies,
I only say, this is the way it is.

Now you will want to see your room,
I dare say . . .
This place gets more like the world
Every day
(It is not forbidden to bandy
Jokes of a general nature
During a conversazione!).
Did you notice how I said "every day"?

ETERNITY

I can see it now,
Sitting there, next to the Doctor
Listening to Berlioz' *Damnation*
Then discussing it at length.

Latini will have something to say
You can be sure
On being ahead of one's time.

Don Juan on Mortuary Art
And the Burden of the Past.
The Old Man's recension of Milton:
Ancient Crux and New Light.

The Case of the Fallen Angel —
Was He Pushed?
A symposium led by Belial.

And the occasional guest speaker:
Jesus on The Harrowing —
Did It Really Work?

There is no end to torments,
The old can be used again and again.
It's in the other place
The programme is a problem.
Heaven help them.

SPOONS

In the *Times Literary Supplement*
Dr Anon is discussing
"Total metaphysical despair".

As when writing, it might be,
And your ballpoint runs dry, or
The typewriter jams in mid-thought.

Total is a lot, though,
And it might last.
Near-total will do for us.

On the edge of one's chair
One can almost tell what totality is,
Or would be.

Perhaps recalling
A wordless creature in a waste lot
In Japan, years ago,
Or other things (it seems) that
Are literally unspeakable
After all, after all.

I can see why they sup with Satan,
Some folk, with their long spoons —
But this man-about-the-cafés
Has an odd way with the cutlery.

"The horror, the horror" —
I could no longer blame Conrad
For his feeble words.
Sometimes it is necessary
That the typewriter jams.

SMALL ORATORIO

Let there be pie
In the sky
When I die

In the sky
Let there be pie

There's nothing shameful in my cry!
If not for pie
What purpose in the sky?

On earth
A dearth

Whate'er his worth
That he will die
Man knows from birth

Let there be pie
Why else a sky?

THE WINE LIST

"—And Paradiso? Is there a paradise?
—I think so, madam,
but nobody wants sweet wines any more."
(Eugenio Montale, trans. G. Singh)

Not so fast, waiter.
If there are those who like sweet wine
And have earned the price of it,
Then they should have it.

Plonk will do for me.
If there's cork in it
Or lipstick on the rim,
I shan't make a fuss.
Some of us will be lucky to get vinegar
Pushed at us.

But for others
You had better be ready to serve sweet wine
In clean glasses, unchipped,
And without a speech.
Some customers are by definition
Right,
And do not require to be told
About a fine dry wine
Deriving from individually crushed grapes
Grown on a certain slope on a small hill
Overlooking a distinguished river.

Some of your customers
Have already been individually crushed.
They know dryness in the mouth,
A harsh taste at the back of the throat.
If sweet wine is what they fancy
You will give them sweet wine.

29

And there should be room on your tray
For ginger beer, orangeade, cocoa, tea
And even the vulgar vintage of colas.

R-AND-R
An Incident from the Vietnam War

We built a palace for them, made of bedrooms.
We even tracked down playmates for them
(No easy job since prostitutes died out
When Independence came). We dug a pool,
Constructed shops, and a hut for movies
With benches outside for the girls to wait on.
Serene House was what we called it.
We did our bit in that war.

Air America flew them in from the battlefield.
We lifted the girls from the suburbs by buses:
Chinese, Indian, Malay, Eurasian,
Playful well-fed girls with lots of life.

There were cameras in plenty, tape-recorders
And binoculars for the soldiers to buy
For the girls; for the girls to sell back
To the shops; for the shops to sell to the soldiers.

Serene House was near the varsity. The G.I.s
Strayed across the campus with Nikons and blank faces.
It was feared they might assault the female students:
The question didn't arise. They seemed scared
Of their own cameras. They looked at nobody,
And nobody looked at them.
                              That war down the road —
It was good for business, and we did our bit.
Otherwise it was a vulgar subject.

Once I found a G.I. in the corridor,
Young and dazed, gazing at the notice-boards.
The Misses Menon, Lee, Fernandez, Poh and Noor
Should report for a tutorial at 3 p.m.
Bringing their copies of *The Revenger's Tragedy*.
If Mr Sharma fails to pass his essay up this week
He will be in serious trouble.
The Literary Society seeks help in cutting sandwiches.

31

He was still there an hour later,
A stunned calf. I asked if I could help.
He shrank away: "Is it not allowed to stand here?"
The corridor was dingy, walls streaked with bat shit,
Somewhere a typewriter clacked like small arms.
"Is there . . . would there be a . . . library?"
One of the best in fact in South-East Asia.
I offered to show him. He trembled
With a furtive pleasure. His only licence
Was to kill, to copulate and purchase cameras.

What sort of books would he like to see?
Out there in the quad he was jumpy,
As if unused to the open. He glanced behind,
Then whispered. Yes, there was something . . .
Did I think . . .

What could he be after? The Natural History
Of the Poontang, with Plates, by some defrocked
Medico called Aristotle? How to Get to Sweden
By Kontiki through the Indian Ocean?

"Would they have anything . . ." A quick look
Round. ". . . by Cardinal Newman, do you think?"
I left him standing there, the *Apologia* in his hands,
He didn't notice when I went away.

Inside Serene House, meanwhile,
All those girls (such lengths we went to!)
Lolled on the benches, played with binoculars,
Clicked their empty cameras, and groused.
The soldiers were glad to get out of Vietnam;
Five days with us and they were happy to go back,
Rest and recreation, they said, was too much for them.
We weren't surprised when the Americans didn't win.

HANDS OFF, FOREIGN DEVIL

Recounting softly some small
Tortuous oriental sorrow,
With dainty Chinese finger-tip
She crushes one by one the ants

Advancing on the office sugar.
Absorbed in her dilemma, trifling
And enormous, the typist deftly
Rubs the ants out one by one.

I turn towards the window,
Listening to her, but not looking,
Not lecturing. The country's hers,
Not mine. The ants too, I suppose.

This here is a Person It is not for
Screwing or soft-soaping or scratching your back against
It is not for weeping on (it hates all kinds of wetness)
Nor will you be permitted to do things to it in the dark
Of a dance hall or a side-street or when it is not looking
Because it is always looking This is a young Person here
It will do what it is asked to do if it approves the request
But otherwise otherwise It has a mind of its own a body of
Its own and above all this Person has a person of its own
And of nobody else It holds views which are its own views
And not necessarily those of the majority or the minority
And all its views are pronounced and it pronounces them all
For this Person is fearless and not afraid to say so because
It believes in absolute honesty to its person and will readily
Exchange opinions on a variety of topics ranging from the
Pollination of orchids through the Poems of Keats to the
Five Sacred Appurtenances of the Sikhs It loves its family
But it is a Person and reserves the right to disagree quite
Radically with its father and mother and brother and sister
It is (it tells you again) a Person and a Person is something
Which many people are not whether in the dark of a dance hall
Or the bosom of a family it remains a Person and is only
Concerned to do what this Person considers right and not to do
What this Person considers wrong

                           And naturally one approves of people
Being Persons especially in the Eastern society to which
This person hardly seems to belong and one is obliged to
Say so and what's more in a tone of admiration For it is
True that not every person appears to be exactly a Person
And it is splendid that this person should stand on its
Own two feet (does it have only two feet? One doesn't dare
To seem to stare) for *being a Person* in fact is the burden of
Much of one's day to day teaching from year to year so truly
One ought to be happy and pleased to hear that this here is a
Person at last Yet Goodbye one says smiling feeling a little
Diminished and unsure of one's own little person and not too
Proud as one thinks of one's one and only little joke when

34

One asked Did it say it was a Parson? And one fears that
In the dark of a dance hall or the bosom of a family or among
The limbs of strangers this Person may be going to be a rather
Lonely person Yet Goodbye one says and perhaps after all
God will be with this Person

OUTSTATION

Standard fans with streamlined dials and
Odd skills, refrigerators with gadgets,
Muzak or TV, and far-fetched liquors
Like Marie Brizard or Bols Apricot —
I like these in the jungle,
The jungle is where they belong.
Grained panels of plastic wood,
Soap-dispensers and pink telephones —
The jungle is where they belong,
They were made for the jungle.
Only extremes should meet,
Without contraries there is no progress.

HOME AND COLONIAL
Henri Rousseau's "Tropical Storm with Tiger"

I'm not one of those simpletons who believe
That if only they had a larger TV screen
They would be able to see the naughty bits.
But if that picture were a few inches longer,
Here on the right-hand side, I mean — then
In fact you would see — not a naughty bit —
You would see me.

Sexual behaviour does exist in the tropics —
Oh indeed — but it's relatively invisible.
It doesn't go on in public. And it wouldn't
Even if there weren't a storm, even if
The jungle weren't so full of spiky things.

Public sex is less sex than public, I reckon.
Like that young couple in the Underground
The other night. They weren't doing anything,
They were simulating it. In my day
We used to dissimulate. And likewise I doubt
This notion that a wider screen creates
A broader mind. What you can see is never
The interesting part. Though of course
I'm not referring to a gentleman like you
Looking at a picture like this
In a reputable gallery.

Imagination is allowed some latitude,
I know (though, as it happens, this painting
Doesn't get enough), but all the same . . .
The jungle's not half as pretty as it looks here,
Untidy at the best, storm or no storm.
The bougainvillaea was tatty and blotched,
Not right out of a hothouse. It was gloomy —
That's another thing about jungles — and
The lightning had that lost air it always has
In those parts. Fumbling around for something

To get a grip on, like a roof, a chimney
Or a golf-club.

But the tiger — Frenchy's hit it off to a T!
Scared stiff, what with its tail behind, which it
Took for a flying snake, and in front — a hairy
Red-faced white man in a post-impressionist sarong,
Heading for the nearest *kedai*.
I fancied an ice-cold Guinness. A moment later
And there'd have been just me on that canvas,
Dry and wet at once, sarong slipping a bit,
Tiger a mile away and still running.

Even so, would you really see more on a larger screen,
D'you think? Or do the girls wear towels or something?

WHO KILLED INNOCENT AMUSEMENT?

When foreigners invaded their land, the Japanese
Were much shocked by the public displays of affection.
When they saw a couple kissing, in their imagination
They were forced to witness the unfolding of the sexual act
Right then and there, to the bitter end.

Even though it might be a gristled American missionary
Kissing his aged mother goodbye on Karuizawa Station.

It was at this time that another foreign invention
Became immensely popular. Japanese gentlemen flocked
To the new striptease theatres. There was no suggestion
That *sutorippu* was suggestive of the rest of the sexual act
Right then and there, to the bitter end.

I often wondered at the discrepancy. But now, suddenly
It dawns upon me that what in their imagination the patrons
Of *sutorippu* witnessed was simply themselves getting into
A respectable public bath and relaxing deliciously.
A far cry from fornicating on Karuizawa Station.

This explanation I find satisfying, and suspect that
Somewhere in the vicinity is a possibly enlightening moral.
But I know that someone will come along at any moment
And tell me I have completely misunderstood the Japanese
Character, or even human nature. Have I for instance
Established a meaningful statistic relationship between
The anti-kissers and the pro-strippers? And they will
Put me down with hard sociological words.

The world is full of trained destroyers and overpaid spoilsports.
Our dear child Innocent Amusement — can she be dead already?

Do you know that land? —
Where the nocturnal tiger
Empties the rubbish bins,

Where the deathless mosquito
Stings the flesh to life
And the body runs with oils!

This splendid desk of teak
I brought from that lost land,
Large, larger than my room —

Now in this temperate clime
Cracks have run across it,
Large, larger everyday.

My nails slipped through them,
Then my fingers — next
My typewriter . . .

If you change your country
Change while you are young,
Before your bones grow brittle
And your life cracks across.

These suburbs of the West,
Dog-haunted, dream
Of soap powders, and the wind
Empties the rubbish bins . . .

Maybe you should try the moon
— You cracked old man —
Once they dust it down.

THE PROGRESS OF POESY

I too would avail myself of the large and common
      benefits of modern technology.

That on the Wings of Imagination a chartered jet
      shall transport me to my inspiration.

That tapes may record the best and happiest moments
      of the happiest and best minds.

That a fine excess of surprising subject-matter
      be relayed to me by satellite.

That powerful pumps ensure the spontaneous overflow
      of powerful feelings.

That cameras shall arrest the vanishing apparitions
      which haunt the interlunations of life.

That sophisticated computers select the best words
      and collocate them in the best order.

*

A pointed stick, some vegetable dye, a strip of bark
      removed by stealth from the public park.

THE PROGRESS OF PRYING

It was while living in Nice
That she began the diaries called
"The Nice Diaries".

Now that "The Nasty Diaries"
Have been discovered
In an attic in Norfolk
We know what "Nice" means.

We know of course what "Nasty" means.
Although her penmanship is such
That editors have not yet established
A definitive text,
We know that "Nasty"
Is not a lake in Finland.

Floods of light are about to be cast
Where hitherto there was no darkness.

THE PROGRESS OF MYTHOLOGY

The high ones speak without hesitation on all things.
Though statecraft be their care or the music of the spheres
Yet they deign to interpret the vying of athletes.
The human heart holds no secrets for them. Unlike ours,
Their second thoughts do not drive out their first.
Self-doubt they know is the seed of the fall of temples.
Their opinions are black and white, and the pale cast
Of thought shall never rob them of their colour.
Our imperfections are not in them. The angry pimple
Does not defile the lucid skin. Their noses do not run.
Sometimes a sacred ichor shines briefly on their brows.
When their voices are raised in debate, it seems
That thunder approaches, and we cower in our huts.
Yet it is rare for immortals to destroy one another.
I shall not name them, for they are household names,
And because these great beings wax exceedingly wroth
If their names are taken in vain, and exact large oblations
In recompense. When we fall at their feet
We try not to tread on their toes. Hyperaesthesia
Is the first infirmity of noble mind. Fame is a spur.
Sometimes they walk among us, and are not recognized
Or are taken one for another. On feast days they visit
Our places of merriment, attired in simple garb,
As they instruct a youthful virgin in the mysteries
Or converse on high matters with the agents of their power.
That they may taste of the common lot and turn it to honey
They have been known to enter our public vehicles.
Intercourse is unwise, however. Remember Ixion
Who embraced a cloud and burned his fingers.
At times I think we are less than worthy of them,
Yet it is said they created us for their pleasure.

OYSTER LAMENT

We are a poor people, who
Cannot afford oysters any more.
The sea is a long way away
Nowadays.

Freedom we have in plenty,
Golden and tall it waves in the fields.
How lovingly somebody tilled the soil,
Manured it so richly!

But who can eat that much? What happened
To those overseas markets? Something is wrong
With the rate of exchange.

It makes such a rattle against the panes.
It is cracking the tarmac out in the streets.
They say it uses up the oxygen.

Freedom is a pearl, to be sure,
A pearl above price.
But so are oysters.
Often I think I would rather have oysters,
Their taste, their indefinable taste.

HISTORY

All in darkness, a sealed train speeds
Through Southfields, a village station.
It is destined for Waterloo,
It has come from Wimbledon.

What bearded brain does it bear?
Or what rough beast might it carry?
A dozen of us, fairly honest workers,
Are left at the platform's edge looking silly.

The field outside my window
Is a bridal suite for dogs.
Their owners enclose them
In the morning and release them
At lunch-time.
Alas there are no curtains.

The ineptitude of virgin dogs!
Dogs have no marriage manuals
Sex they know but not always gender.
But they live up to their name
Try, try and try again.
At noon they are taken home exhausted.

In the afternoon
The field outside my window
Is a football pitch for boys.
I could wish there were curtains.

The ineptitude of playing boys!
When the ball bounces off them
They fall to the ground.
But they live up to their name
They rise and rise again.
At tea-time they are taken home exhausted.

Whatever may befall the Old Country
(And sometimes I fear it will)
Of dogs and footballers
There shall never be a poverty.

A COMMON INTEREST

What is needed is a common interest,
What you might call a friendly rivalry.

My wife is patron of the cat,
I am patron of the dog.
The cat and the dog are not exactly friends,
In fact they lead a rather turbulent life.

My wife backs the cat and I support the dog.
She fattens the cat and keeps its claws in trim,
I teach the dog a trick or two.

She has equipped her client with sparklers
To brandish in its mouth.
I tell her, Peace Prizes have come from gunpowder.
We laugh. Then I teach my protégé to spit.

An atomic pellet placed in the cat's saucer?
We discuss it sensibly, and agree
To avoid any serious damage to the house.
After all, we live in it.

I think she is training the cat to drop things
From a height.
I shall fit the dog out with a helmet
And file its teeth.

How the fur flies!

We live in perfect amity, my wife and I,
Our marriage is founded on a rock.

UNDERGROUND MOVEMENTS

Computers Need People

They are advertising for people
In the Underground.
A good place for it, you still find people
In the Underground.

The train drivers are practically all
Coloured computers these days.
Should coloured computers get jobs
That white people could do equally well?

It takes a computer to work out
The rights and wrongs of these questions.

People Need Love

   "Are you sitting opposite
   The new man in your life?"

Or is it that because of the people
Strap-hanging between, you cannot see
The man who is sitting opposite and
Might have been the new man in your life?

Can it be you are not sitting opposite
The man who would have been the new man
In your life because he failed to fight
His way onto the train at the last station?

Is neither of you sitting opposite anyone
And is your heel digging into the sensitive
Instep of the person who will never be,
Not now, the new man in your life?

Or is the person who could have been
The new man in your life, is he
About to strangle the life out of you
Because you are crushing him to death?

We would not ask such difficult questions
Of innocent and well-meaning computers
Were it not that they have offered
To answer our difficult questions.

IMPROVING POEM FOR CHILDREN

The cat sits on the mat.
He miaows. He would like to go out.
He had better stay in. The world outside
Is full of dirty dogs.

I think of a world where we all
Would do whatever we liked.
And whatever we liked to do
Would be liked by everyone else.
And what everyone else liked to do
Would be liked by us. All the time.

The cat continues to miaow.
If I let him out
He will sit on the mat outside
And miaow to come in.
Inside and out the world is full
Of dirty dogs and querulous cats.

For a moment I sit on my chair,
I hear the miaowing, I hear the barking,
And I feel like God. Uneasy.
I think of choice and necessity,
The spiritual wants of the feline creation
And of all the others.
I think I have made a mistake.

The cat sits on the mat.
He continues to yowl.
I sit on my chair and scowl.
No one is doing what he likes.

OR PERCHANCE NOT

Work — say I, coining a phrase
In the firm's money — is the
Curse of the dreaming classes.
It makes me sleep like the dead.
Where are they now, those bright
And fearful dreams I used to live?
Ingenious phantoms who conveyed
So much reality?

Dreaming will have to stop —
So says reality, aggrieved,
Wet blanket on my bed,
The tired dog in my manger.
I work, therefore for tax and
Other purposes, I am.
Then I sleep the sleep of the just,
Which is death.

FELLOWSHIP

Even cheap wine is dear.
Most of his books sold approximately
One copy each, last year.
But must have something to offer.

There's a wary footfall on the stair.
The young Fellow from the States is here,
To study him and his work, in the light
Of the plight . . . On a travel grant
Right to the top of that hazardous flight.

"*Doch was fördert es mich* —
But what use to me, that the careful Chinee
Has painted on glass both Werther and Lottie?"

Deserves a drink, though. Quite probably
It was he who bought those books last year,
Or persuaded some library.

What was that phrase we used to hear
In those old-time Shakespeare courses? —
"The inversion of the natural order".
A bad thing, sure. To what did it allude?
Oh yes, horses eating other horses.

"I'm sorry about the wine . . ."
Sorrier still if he's expecting food.

THE CAULDRON

"it is the time when uprightly and in pious
sober wise, naught of work is to be wrought
and art grown unpossible without the divel's
help and fires of hell under the cauldron . . ."

It had grown impossible
Very little work was getting done.
So we gave up sobriety
The other virtues as well
(We supposed that once we had them)
And we stoked the fires of hell.

How we stoked them! It was fun at first
At first there were virgins to astound
There were things to be done with things
There were things to be done in private
There were things to be done in public
At first.

It was style we believed in, not the devil
It was the devil we got.
The fires of hell are not for hire
Without the ice.
There was a saying about the devil . . .
But memory has gone, we killed it
A package deal.

Now there is no one to astound
The devil only laughs at his own jokes
Us he finds boring.
There is nothing to do in public
Nothing to do in private.
Under the dry cauldron icy fires are burning
Art is grown impossible.

Where is the future? Nothing stirring
Unless a memory stirs.
Wasn't there an ancient saying . . .
About a time when uprightly alone
In pious sober wise can work be done
And with the devil's hindrance?

OF GROWING OLD

They tell you of the horny carapace
Of age,
But not of thin skin growing thinner,
As if it's wearing out.

They say, when something happens
For the sixth or seventh time
It does not touch you. Yet
You find that each time's still the first.

To know more isn't to forgive more,
But to fear more, knowing more to fear.
Memory it seems is entering its prime,
Its lusty manhood. Or else

Virility of too-ripe cheese —
One can mature excessively,
And there's another name for that.
Give me cheese-tasters for psychiatrists!

Of growing old
Lots of kindly things have been reported.
Surprising that so few are true.
Is this a matter for complaint? I don't know.

THE AGEING POET

The Ageing Poet is a fertile subject for an Ageing Poet.
He knows an awful lot about it. He will relate
How the Ageing Poet's teeth are falling out (in fact
They fell out long ago, when he was a Younger Poet)
And also his hairs, as absolute as falling hopes
(An image coined in youth to point a contrary moral).
Policemen, he observes, are for ever getting younger,
Along with publishers, prime ministers and undertakers.
He may in these tolerant times remark on how a miniskirt
Or even a gymslip produces a brief but distinct convulsion
In his sluggish blood — a touchingly autumnal yearning,
Whatever the Poet himself may concurrently be up to.
(One expects to do a little better than one's fictions.)
Death too is an aspect of the human condition which may
Properly be tackled now. Mere conceit in a Young Poet,
In an Ageing Poet it testifies to courage and realism.
Also he has a number of dead friends, some quite famous,
He can mention in passing. Timor mortis is beyond reproach.

The Young and the Younger Poet may still have his teeth,
And his hairs, and his hopes that before much longer
These tedious Ageing Poets will turn into Dead ones.
He may have access to miniskirts or (come to that) gymslips,
Not to mention abortion, divorce and idealism.
But the Ageing Poet is better off. He has himself, all of him.
For a little while longer, a book or two more.

A COMMUTER'S TALE

A little late, but still in time
For the end of *Z Cars*,
After a drink in town with a friend,
On the last lap
The road downhill from the Tube,
Puffing at your pipe, puffing
At yourself too.

Just at the bend, and almost home,
A — what? — a curious behaviour
In the chest, a rush-hour press
And stab of bodies, elbows, feet.

Well, at your age not unheard of
(Nor unread of, every morning),
Yet oddly, no embarrassment
(Must thank the drink for that)
At what portends a sorry solecism,
An exhibition you were brought up
Not to make.
But even some amusement
(Childish, suited to a childish mood)
As you remember:
Your season ticket, it expires today.

VACILLATIONS OF AN ASPIRING VAMPIRE

"Guaranteed and proven," said Rousseau,
A man of reason. "The evidence is complete."

I shall wear two fine pointed teeth
And a charming manner.
The ladies will be dressed in décolletage.
Nothing's more taking than necks and breasts.
The tooth is nearer to the nerve-centre,
The mouth is nearer to the heart.
This is the height of intimacy,
The rest is low and brutish.

It means a lot, when all your life
You've lacked both power and charm.
The tonics they gave me as a child
Did nothing for the blood.
My teeth are made of chalk.
I was weaned too soon by far.
I have had trouble with bras.

"The testimony of persons of quality,"
Said Rousseau. "Surgeons, priests and judges."

But the laws require a tooth for a tooth.
I must be hospitable to strangers,
I shall have to give up garlic
And hide away the rood that came from Lourdes.
For first I too must die beneath the charmer's lips.

And even then, how short-lived
Immortality can be!
I see a cross nestling between full breasts,
I see myself unseen in a mirror,
I see a policeman bearing a pointed stake.

I fear those persons of quality,
Those surgeons, priests and judges,
And also the patrons of cinemas.
You could lose what little blood you have.

PERFECT LOVE

I am in love with Lady X
Whose statue stands in the market place
(Not with Lord X: I am not unnatural).

Although for many a year
Sore circumstance has come between us
(She is married to another).

Cruel pressures can deform true lovers,
Turn the sweet to sour, and twist
The upright.

Yet she remains as noble as ever.
Which is why I continue to love
The statue of Lady X in the market place.

Long sorrows have not left their mark
On Lady X in the market place,
Nor on me who loves her.

SYMPOSIUM

The Ancients found something to be said
On both sides.
Though not so desirable as boys,
Women continued to be desirable (if less so)
For rather longer.
Marriage, it was finally agreed,
Was a useful institution without which
There might be neither boys nor girls.
However, women smeared themselves
With disgusting unguents,
Whereas a boy had a simple splash in the morning
And led a clean life.
The general view was that the wise man
Chose pederasty, on the grounds that
Perfect virtue is not found in women.

Some doubted it was found in boys either.
Hence perhaps arose the love of God,
Who is not always with us,
The perfection of whose virtue is less debatable.

Meanwhile the citizens did their utmost
To lead a full life,
Impeded only by poverty, war and sickness,
And the perversity of boys and girls and gods.

LITERARY PARTY

No end of handsome women around,
Some of them influential. And men
With pull in the media — the press,
The BBC, the NBL, the PEN,
Rebels with big purses, or else big breasts.
We move from usefulness to beauty,
Here a commission, phone number there,
Promise of a mention, promise of a promise . . .
In short, a first-rate party.

There was a female earlier on, drably
Dressed, no one knew her, of little use
You'd say, and certainly no beauty.
She gulped a glass or two of wine
In a corner, mumbling something strange.
Now someone's saying, she was the Muse,
And went off with a sour look on her face.
But a night's sleep will do the trick.
Tomorrow she'll feel better. Things won't change.

BUY ONE NOW

This is a new sort of Poem,
It is Biological.
It contains a special Ingredient
(Pat. pend.) which makes it different
From other brands of poem on the market.

This new Poem does the work for you.
Just drop your mind into it
And leave it to soak
While you relax with the telly
Or go out to the pub
Or (if that is what you like)
You read a book.

It does the work for you
While (if that is what you like)
You sleep. For it is Biological
(Pat. pend.), it penetrates
Into the darkest recesses,
It removes the understains
Which it is difficult for us
Even to speak of.

Its action is so gentle
That the most delicate mind is unharmed.
This new sort of Poem
Contains an exclusive new Ingredient
(Known only to every jackass in the trade)
And can be found in practically any magazine
You care to mention.

If you write for children
Perhaps grown-ups will read you
(Don't forget the great peut-être).

But write for adults,
Only posterity will read you
(For all that you can tell).

The world has slipped a generation.
It seems the flames burn low
Beneath its groaning cauldron.

Regard *Biography*, "the line that sells".
When heroes sink to men, then
What can men sink to? Voyous, voyeurs.

So write for him who always listens —
Stewing in your juicy brain-pan,
Every man his own small pyramid.